Destiny Nearly Aborted

VICTORENE FOSTER KELLEM

DESTINY NEARLY ABORTED
Victorene Foster Kellem

Published by Pecan Tree Publishing

Hollywood, FL 33020

www.pecantreebooks.com

info@pecantreebooks.com

Paperback ISBN: 979-8-9855014-7-6

E-book ISBN: 979-8-9855014-8-3

Library of Congress Control Number: 2022905769

Pecan Tree Publishing
www.pecantreebooks.com

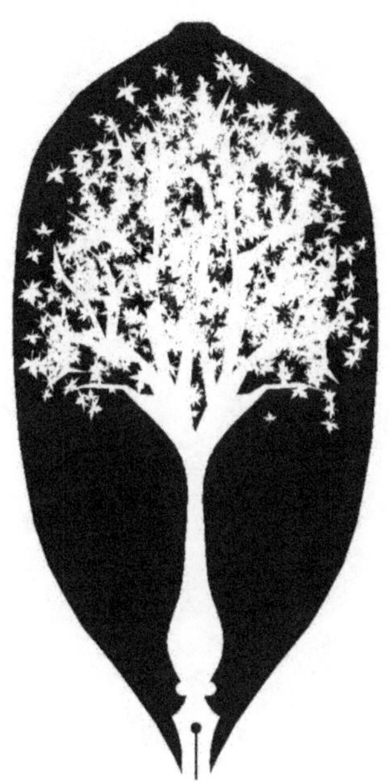

New Voices | New Styles | New Vision
Creating a New Legacy of Dynamic Authors and Titles
Hollywood, FL

Dedication

I dedicate this book to my parents, Lorette Arletha Veronica Johnson Foster and Curtis Cane Ellis, and my stepfather Luther Foster. They loved me the only way they knew how to. Their lives were filled with misunderstandings, misfortunes, and mistakes. Because of their lack of knowledge about the necessity to know themselves, and the ones from whom they came, they experienced so much pain. Because they did, I had to learn what it took to be a whole, happy, "free from bondage" woman. And I learned that being the absolute best version of myself was all I need to be. How blessed I am now to know who holds my past, present and future. And it is God, alone.

To my children and grandchildren, thank you for loving me, despite all my flawed attempts to be the perfect mother and grandmother (G-Mommy). I made bad choices which only showed my imperfections. Live your life on your own terms and by the Word of God. It's okay to change your mind, especially if you find you made the wrong choice! Take what you need from this life and give back what God requires of you. Please believe that I did what I thought to be right at the time. I love you all.

To my siblings, who seemed to look up to me but in reality, it was me who looked up to them. I was always too afraid to really venture out into the world. It wasn't that I was so saved, but I was too scared to try. I love you all more now than ever before. This may bring you pain for a moment, and for that, I'm deeply sorry. But as time moves forward, I hope you understand it was necessary for me. I also pray this book will bring understanding and closure to you as it did for me.

To the late, but great, Pastor Olla B. Haynes, who was my first real connection to the Lord. She was more than just a pastor to me; she was a grandmother to me and a mother to my mother. The first person that I can remember praying for me. Even when I disappointed her and didn't listen to her wisdom and guidance, she didn't give up on me. Pastor Haynes was still there loving and praying and holding me up before the Lord.

To the late Pastor Rickey A. Tates Sr. and Lady Madlyn L. Tates. There are not enough words to express my appreciation for your support throughout the years. Pastor Tates was a father to my children when they were fatherless. A big brother to me when I needed one. He believed and encouraged me when I didn't believe in myself. He nurtured and pushed me into my purpose and ministry, instilling a spirit of excellence in me in the process. He urged me to always do my best in everything and never act half-heartedly. I still carry that spirit to this day in everything I do.

To Lady Tates, who promised to be a friend to me. At a time when I felt like I didn't have anyone in the world, she was there and so much more. Her passing was heartbreaking for me. I will always remember the wonderful times we shared, as family to my children and me. Blessings, love, and happiness to the family she left to carry on her legacy!

To my cousin's mother, who always loved me just as I was, flawed and broken. I never had to try to be something or someone I wasn't with you. You would always say, "You don't have to change anything for me to love you, but if you are going to see God, that's when change has to come!" Thank you for setting an example of a true Godly woman and always speaking the truth. You believed in me when I didn't believe in myself and kept me encouraged.

To my incredibly special aunt Rita, who inspired me my whole life to be a giver, and now a writer. I pray that God will give you all that you deserve in this life and the one to come. Don't give up on doing good and what's right! Know that God sees all and knows all, and it is He who will reward you in the end.

To Aunt Linda, you don't know how much that letter you saved all those years ago, means to my sisters and myself. A letter from our mother, in her own handwriting expressing her love for us. It was right on time!

Thank you, Aunt Donna and Aunt Vickie, your visit to my house was such a blessing to our family. My granddaughter still talks about you. The "mad money" blessing you put under my pillow, was right on time for me. It was one of the sweetest things anyone has ever done for me.

Aunt Gloria, I love you so much. Thank you for thinking of me and giving me some of the things that my mother gave my grandmother. Knowing they were no longer with us, made each item doubly special.

To some special cousins, who are like big sisters to me and helped me through an exceedingly difficult time in my life. I love and appreciate all of you very much!

To Pastor Vera Woods, my pastor, cousin, sister, and my friend. I don't think I would have made it without you to hold me up before the Lord in prayer, and in so many other supportive ways. The example of courage and unwavering faith you've shown in times of trouble and heartaches has been incredible. You've been through the storm and the rain, yet you are still standing. The support you gave me during the time of my mother's death I will never forget or be able to repay. I thank the almighty God for you and your wisdom at a time when I was feeling so lost and alone.

To my former bishop, Wade E. Harris, I didn't think I would ever find another pastor as giving as the late

Pastor Rickey Tates, and then you came along. Thank you for all you have done for my family and myself. Love is not what you say, but what you do, I appreciate you.

And to the rest of my family and friends, as you read this, call out your own name (if the shoe fits). I thank each of you for what you have done for me in my life. The good, the bad and the ugly. You have played an important part in me becoming the woman I am today. I didn't understand nor was I willing to embrace it at the time, but everything that happened got me to where I am today. May God keep His hand over your lives!

I've saved the best for last! To the one true love of my life, a man sent from God specifically for me. My best friend, my lover, my bishop, and pastor, thank you for your support and constant confidence in my abilities even when I doubted myself. You are the man I have been waiting on for 25 years. I love the way you love me when you love me and how you love me! Thank you, Jesus, for Apostle James Edward Kellem!

This book may not be a pleasurable read for some, but it is true. To change and move forward in this life, I had to deal with the truth! And sometimes the truth hurts; sometimes it's embarrassing and hard to deal with. But it's necessary for growth, forgiveness, and freedom. When you understand that, only the truth can truly set you free, (Biblically and naturally), then you will be free in your spirit and life! I love you all.

My Purpose

I'm sharing my story to help my family set themselves free, as well as others, who may have found themselves in similar situations, to be set free. But most of all, sharing my story to set my own soul free of the bondage of shame and generational curses. I need to be free from me, for me! When you talk about the trauma of your mistakes, sins, and generational curses, only then you can truly be free. If you want to be happy and free, you must face yourself, your sins, and your fears. Confess where you are; you may not always like what you'll see, but it is your truth to own. If you want to move forward and be free from the chains of sin and shame and help others, you must become truthful and transparent. If you want to be used by God, you must speak truth and not only the Word of God. You must not speak just someone else's truth but your own truth. By the time I'm done facing myself, my fears, pains, hurts, mistakes, and my sins, I expect to become the best version of myself I can be. God deserves a better me! The best me. A stronger me. A wiser me - free of the bondage of sin and shame! This imitation of me has held me captive. I have always been a very private individual, but the writing of this book has caused me to pull back the covers off my life and raise the shades on my windows, leaving me in full view to the world.

Victorene Foster-Kellem

Table of Contents

Chapter 1

Understanding the Woman

What do you see when you look in the mirror? While your physical attributes have value, do they represent the total woman or man? Do you see more? Are you satisfied or content with what appears to your natural eye? There is more to you than what you see in the mirror. That's what I felt about myself. The real me cannot be seen with the natural eye, only with the heart and a spiritual eye. Through those lenses she appears and can be seen.

I thought I knew who I was. I saw myself as a person with good moral values and someone you could depend on in a time of need. Yes, these things were true, but there was more. I found myself doing and saying things that I never thought I would. I committed acts of sin and betrayal that I never imagined I was capable of. Some of my acts were against people I said I loved or at least cared deeply about. Lurking in the shadows of my mind was a dark side. A side that did not want to live as a Christian. That part of me was against everything good and morally ethical. That was the kind of darkness I did not want to believe existed in me. But it did, Paul wrote in Romans 7:9, "For the good that I would I do not: but the evil which I would not, that I do." (KJV) That was the way I felt constantly. I was fighting with evil thoughts and deeds, while wanting to be good and do good. As much as I tried to do right, I was still willing to do anything to satisfy the darker side of myself.

There were missing pieces, and this left me with uncontrollable desires that laid deep within. I often though if I identified them, I could have exercised better self-control over my flesh and avoided many potholes and painful experiences. But how can you understand yourself if you don't know yourself? These acts of betrayal brought guilt and shame. It wasn't like I didn't know what I was doing wrong, because I did, but I didn't care. I believe the concept of people who are hurt turn around and hurt others to be true. When people are repeatedly hurt, especially by those whom they put trust in, it causes a foundation of distrust to form. After that foundation of distrust solidifies, the walls begin to build up around you. The wall of deceit, the wall of manipulation, the wall of hidden agendas, and the wall of distance. When all the walls are completely up, the roof goes on. I call it the roof of self-preservation. At this point you do not trust anyone, and you always feel you are being lied to. As a result, you are always on your guard. You suspect everyone has a hidden agenda, and nobody says what they mean. Keeping your distance from others is your safety net. Even your loved ones are kept out your inner circle. All this to protect yourself from hurt.

That was me. I built that type of house for my children and me. The home I made for us had no trust; and no genuine loving affection was shown. I hurt them mentally and emotionally by cutting them off from the physical and emotional love of their mother. As babies, it was easy to hold and kiss their little heads. It was easy to play with their little fingers and sing to them as they fell asleep, but when they became toddlers that natural loving connection started to fade. By the time they were in grade school, it was gone. They grew up and became someone I had to protect myself from. I was afraid to get close to my own children! I had trapped myself in the house I built. Getting to know yourself is more than looking in the mirror and judging what one might see. It's not just about the color of your skin, the shape or color of your eyes, or the texture of your hair, or even being fat or thin, short or tall. While those are a part of our physical being, they are not the total definition of whom you are. They were not the total definition of who I am! There was more to me than that; and more to you.

Understanding what and who you are made up of is the key that opens the door to your real identity. You cannot know who you are, and what your capabilities are, without understanding where or whom you came from and where they came from. Identify what's on the inside of you and who is in control of you. By becoming aware of this then you can determine the next course of action. You get to recognize what is alive and what is dormant, what should be called out, cast out, or activated, and embraced in you. I have an unquenchable desire to know who I am.

When we come to Christ we must be born again. Everything in us must change. The Bible says in Psalms 51:5 (KJV), "Behold, I was shaped in iniquity; and in sin did my mother conceive me." You are born with a sinful nature, which means you are born with a mind to do wrong from the beginning. In Second Corinthians 5:17 (KJV) we find, "Therefore if any man be in Christ, he is a new creature; old things are passed away; behold, all things are become new." That means Christ Jesus can give a clean heart, a right mind, and a renewed spirit in all of us. No longer must we be bound by sin or the bondage that sin carries. Through Christ Jesus, an old vessel can be destroyed and made anew and productive.

As far back as I can remember, my parents have always considered themselves to be the black sheep of their families. Who were my parents organically? My mother, although she had been married four times, spent much of her adult life as a single parent. She was never married to my father. My mother began having children when she was 15. She had me, her second child, at 16. My mother had a variety of mommy issues, she was the oldest of eight children. Raised primarily by her maternal grandmother, she struggled with feelings of abandonment, and being unloved, and unwanted.

My father however, had what I would consider to be a healthy, normal childhood. He was raised in a home with both parents. My grandparents were married and hard workers that provided for their family. My grandparents were both Christians (Church of God in Christ) with high morals and values. My father did not want anything to do with the church or what was right. He was a military man who witnessed horrifying acts of war which left him mentally scarred and emotionally damaged. There were multiple flaws in their character that influenced their troubled souls, emotionally and spiritually. These genetic and generational curses attached themselves to me during my conception. Without knowing it, they had successfully passed their curses to me. Whatever traumas I wasn't born with, became behaviors I learned to survive my environment. The unexplainable behaviors and emotions were different genetic and emotional parts of my parents, who struggled to overcome them, but failed. There was a stranger living inside of me. I had to get to know them to understand myself.

I wish I could tell you after I started on this journey how wonderful it was to finally meet myself and understand things. That everything about me was wonderful, sweet, nice, perfect, and amazing! But that would be far from the truth. Becoming transparent with myself during the process was essential for my complete success. I had been good at seeing through the camouflages of others, but now it was time to see through my own glass-stained windows. I was facing the truth without excuses!

Sometimes you don't want to be honest with yourself. Sugarcoating and half-truths look more desirable and felt safe. I couldn't do that anymore. This had to serve the purpose for which it was intended. I had to be honest and straightforward with myself, as I had been with everybody else; and that was scary and painful. I hurt my own feelings. I made myself cry. I beat myself up. Facing me was agonizing, unpleasant nasty, bitter, heartbreaking, traumatic, disturbing, and uncomfortable.

I faced it in parts. I couldn't do it all at one time. When facing myself, I found out I was very rude, cold, and cut-throat at times. I couldn't understand how I could be so giving and caring and those negative things at the same time. There was so much good inside of me (I thought), but there was another side that was not good. Where could this kind of behavior come from? I had all of this going on inside of me. But there was an explanation that I had never taken into consideration, genetic deoxyribonucleic acid, better known as DNA. Was that it? My parents were at work in me. There was a wealth of DNA history unknown concerning my parents. As I began to search out and reflect on what I knew about them, I saw similar behaviors within myself which shed light on my undesirable character traits.

Over the years I became very impatient. I do not know whether it was because I was worn out from the cares of life; or because I was taking care of three grandchildren and my patience for children was long gone. The expiration date, like the one stamped on a milk carton, has passed! I didn't know what the problem was; but it wasn't an excuse to be that way. It was ugly. My attitude toward my surrounding situations was shameful. I didn't like me anymore. Therefore, how could anyone else like me? There were times it seemed like I was standing outside of my body looking at myself and wondering what I was doing! I would run the questions through my mind. Why are you saying that? Why are you acting that way? Will I always be like this? Was this the end of me? Can I change? Will this always be me?

You see, this is one of the generational curses I had seen in my mother and all the women in our lineage. I was not going to let their end be my end! This was the crossroad for me, something had to change. How or what was I going to do to change? I had no idea, but I knew it would not be easy.

Chapter 2

Acknowledge The Need for Change

Most people are fearful of the change necessary for their lives to be completely successful. We often don't understand that change benefits our lives. Change can often lead to freedom, deliverance, and power. I was living a defeated life without any of these possibilities. It was not until I understood that change would bring me into a prepared purpose of God that I decided to live differently. I decided to live in a place I so desperately wanted to be. A place of wholeness, wellness, and peace with myself and then with others. Once this was aligned, everything else could and would fall into place.

Webster's Dictionary says that change is a noun. "A noun is a word used to identify any class of people, places or things or to name a particular one of these." Webster's definition of change is, "the act or instance of making or becoming different, to take or use another instead of." For example, the change from loose coins to a matching amount of bills. Although it's the same amount of currency, it is in a different form. Through change you can become different although you are the same, with an adjusted or changed mindset. The Bible says in Second Corinthians 5: 17 (KJV) "therefore If any man be in Christ, he is new creature old things are passed away and behold all things become new."

Change is never comfortable and always has a price to be paid by the one in need of it. But anything worth having is worth paying the price for. Jesus paid a price that no one else could pay and Jesus is, our example. Only I can pay the price for my change. Change causes the sacrifice of our will. Change may cause us to walk away from people, places, and things for a season or permanently, but we must remember it's worth it all. Change will bring our relationship to God closer. Change will bring us to a place in God where He can truly use us for His glory as His servant. Once changed, we can be a mouthpiece for His Word, encouragement to the brokenhearted, a teacher – by example - to His people, unconditionally loving to a friend and an enemy, and a whole, healthy, mighty servant of God.

I knew this would never happen without getting to the root of all my issues. By doing this then I could make the changes necessary to tear down and destroy whatever was holding me back so that I could mature in God. I was a partial woman with missing, infected, broken, and inactive pieces, trying to appear to be a whole, healthy, mighty woman of God to the world. I dressed it up with all the fancy clothes, the hats, and the shoes with matching purses, all of which have nothing to do with my soul or God. I even tried to fool myself. It worked for a while, until I wanted more than what I saw.

The idea that I had to be strong for everybody else, needed to change in me. What I needed to understand was, being weak wasn't a terrible thing. It was an alarm clock telling me it was time to look to Jesus. The Word of God says, in Second Corinthians 12:9, "My grace is sufficient for thee: for my strength is made perfect in weakness." (KJV) In my weakness, Jesus is made strong. When I depend on Jesus to take the lead, my strength doesn't matter just my faith. I was going to church Sunday after Sunday wondering why no one saw my pain. I was in the house of the Lord with the all-seeing all-knowing saints of God; yet all they saw was a walking fashion show! Where was their discernment? Why is it that they could not see the hurt, pain, the distance, and lack of love in me or did they care? My pain was invisible to them. I was spiritually broken, and bleeding and they walked right past me like I didn't exist. Was the face I was wearing and the front I portrayed that good? This was all wrong, but who was at fault? Them or me? I had the need for change, I should have been the one to reach out, but my pride stopped me. Was this their fault and lack of discernment? Or was the real problem me not responding to the altar calls following the Word of God, just to keep anyone from knowing the condition or issue I was having at the time. You know you always have those looky-loos who come to church seeking out someone's business. They couldn't wait to hear what you were praying for so they can run back with half a story to tell. But did I want to keep up the illusion that I was alright? Not if I wanted change. Not if I wanted help. All that had to change - in me.

If I wanted help, I was going to have to be willing to put myself out there and let it be known what was going on with me. Yes, I had to put my pride aside. I couldn't afford to be bound by the guilt or the shame of pain any longer. No more pretending like I was living a perfect fairy tale life on the outside, while on the inside there was a constant battle. Finally, at the crossroad, the place of making the decision to surrender my life and my heart to the Lord – change brought hope. Was that all I needed to do? Or was that the beginning of the real fight. You see, they taught me what a church looked like, so I knew how to look like a church! I knew how to dress like a church! I knew how to talk like a church! And I was particularly good at it. I knew what to do, when to do it and how to do it, but that wasn't enough. God requires more. Yes, He wants more of us. He requires a lifestyle that's in alignment with His Word! It is time to take off that church mask, strip off the church look, and deal with what's underneath the church surface.

I wanted the change from the inside out, the change that would bring me to face myself. I wanted to be exposed to my truth. I wanted to know myself and what I needed to do to change. I had to seek the Lord for direction about what would bring me into a place of deliverance. Fasting and praying was His clarion strategy for me to get in the position so that He could do the work in me. In doing this, I was bringing me into His alignment for my life, where the final changes necessary could indwell and my destiny could come into manifestation.

Time ran out for the blame game, holding other people responsible and accountable for what went wrong in my life. I had to take responsibility for my own life and the direction that I wanted to go into. It did not matter how I started out, it does not matter what my mother did or what my father did, or what the church folks did. Who abused me, who raped me, who molested me, who mistreated me, who misunderstood me, did not matter! It was up to me to shift what happened to me. We can choose to accept a defeated life or stand up, fight, and claim the victory of Jesus Christ, who lay down His life for us!

I had been in the church for years. I knew the walk, the talk, and when to raise my hands and say hallelujah. Something was still missing. Missing was a relationship with God that would lead me beyond church walls, church people, church talk and church work. I could not do kingdom work, without a relationship with God. Going to church alone will not give you a relationship with God. The reality had set in and taken hold and I no longer wanted to settle for being a look alike or an imitator. This sister wanted to be healthy, walking and talking in all the power, authority and anointing that God had for her. I knew that all of this was possible, but I was going to have to change my way of thinking. The Bible says in Proverbs 23:7, "For as he thinketh in his heart, so is he" (KJV). The heart of a man lies within the mind of a man. Change begins in the mind. My thinking process became critical. Although my habits and behaviors had not changed yet, I had to change my thinking process. What I thought about, how I thought it, my attitude about myself, all this was important in the process of change. I was in search of the woman God called me to be!

Chapter 3

What's the Issue?

Let me start with the issue no one wants to talk about. It is so much easier to blame others for what is going wrong in life. It is always someone else's fault! But the fact of the matter is our issues are our issues! Life can be complicated at times; making it difficult to see our shortcomings in situations. I could not comprehend this concept either, I was in the right all the time, most of the time, sometimes! But was I really? I had a friend once and we had a good relationship. But we had an issue. We liked to shop and every time we went to the store together, she needed money, and she would say, "Girl I'll give it back to you when I get paid." She never would. I would never ask her about giving me my money back, because after doing this for years, I knew she was not forgetting. She was taking advantage of me, or she thought I was a fool! Either way, after years of enduring her financial abuse, I decided to put a stop to it. One day I said, "No, I don't have it." I was testing whether she would still be a friend since my money was off limits! We remained friends and she started paying for her own purchases. I could put all the wrong on her, but the truth is I should have asked for my money when she did not return it the first time. Blaming others when we refuse to address the situations ourselves is an easy way out of not taking responsibility for our own actions.

The reason most people avoid uncomfortable situations is because they wouldn't have to deal with self-reflection. True? Saying it was my fault, saying I was wrong, saying I'm sorry or asking for forgiveness is too much. Why is it so hard to admit when we're wrong? Pride is the greatest reason. Or could it be unforgiveness? Or both? Both were true for me; but pride by far was the biggest. My pride masqueraded as someone being very private. I was quick to take offense to anyone saying that I was prideful. To me, this meant I was looking sinful, which triggered the unforgiveness part. I told myself I didn't care what people thought about me. That wasn't true at all. I've always wanted the approval of others, especially those close to me. I had a hard shell, but the inner me was tender to the touch, easily broken and offended: and slow to forgive others. We can be so blind to our own issues.

Let me tell you about my ignorance, my pride, and my unforgiveness. Let's discuss me not having the courage to confess or confront my own issues and, my inability to face my weaknesses and failures.

I need to speak about the generational curses and the exposure of ugly secrets. We had men in the family who had no self-control, so they molested me, I'm sure I was not the only one. Our women with such low self-esteem, turned their heads and pretended not to know what was happening to their babies. The incest that was going on, everybody knew about, but nobody did anything to stop! So many lying tongues, made it hard to believe anyone. They were adulterers, sexual abusers, spousal abusers, child neglectors, verbal abusers, drug addicts, gang bangers, and promiscuous women. Mothers and fathers abandoned their children, leaving them to other family members to raise. These issues were the tip of the iceberg. The blood line curse gripped my family like Super Glue™ for generation after generation; and it must be put to death.

The mistakes of my past caused so much shame that I tried to pretend it didn't happen. But it's time to speak out and put an end to it all. I want to be able to help the next generation and I cannot help them if I keep silent. I cannot walk in compassion, empathy or understanding of those who are in the same condition, until I understand and deal with myself – first. Sometimes we try to fix others, with the same issues that we ourselves still have. But you and I must accept that we will never be able to fix ourselves or anyone else, only God can do that! But we can help lead others to The One who can change or fix anyone. But until we get the help we need; we cannot help anyone. And we cannot speak the whole truth about them, until we know the whole truth about us. What I know is half the battle! What I will expect and accept and do with it is the rest! I used to think that however I start out in life, would set the pace for how I would end up in this life. I know now that it does not have to be that way.

I used to weigh over 450 pounds! Until my mother died from all the things that were brought on from her being overweight. You see the weight in her life began to slowly affect every area of her life until it completely consumed her. Her physical, mental, social, financial, health and finally her spiritual life. I was headed down that same path with no way out! I was so miserable and unhappy! I had to decide to live or die! Worrying about what others thought and said cost me my self-esteem. Along with the failed relationships with the fathers of my children, the overeating, and the need for others' approval – I worsened with time. I decided that fat people ran in the family, and I had to be one of them. My mother and my grandmothers on both sides were fat. So was I. I was turning to food for love, comfort, and support instead of dealing with my emotional and physical problems. This led me to being severely overweight, and my life was on the line, I had to do something to save myself. I became deeply desperate, and desperate people do desperate things. I had to get the weight off. I tried diet after diet and failed.

Years prior, I thought about gastric bypass, but I had heard so many dreadful things about it from people that I didn't think it was the best option for me at that time. But when I was desperate, I needed to do something, and I couldn't do it on my own. So, gastric bypass was back on the table. I didn't want to tell anyone because I did not want anyone to try to talk me out of it. Once I decided to do it, I only shared my decision with my son Jermaine, my daughter Arletha and my sister Sandra. When I was going into the hospital for the procedure, I called my cousin Vera and I told her I was going into the hospital. I didn't tell her why, but I asked her not to visit or ask me any questions, but to simply pray for me. I knew that was hard for her, but she respected my wishes. There were other people in the family who had the same surgery and they shared their experiences. But I didn't want anybody watching everything I ate or watching to see how much weight I lost or if I was gaining it back. I wanted my privacy. People can be so judgmental and invade your privacy. I didn't want to deal with any of it or hear about someone who died from having it done.

People tend to think that when you have gastric bypass you don't have to do any work. I think that's one of the misconceptions that didn't get to me because I knew there was still work involved. The surgery was a tool, a booster to get you started, but you must work to keep it off or you can regain what you lost and more. When the weight first began to fall off, I was so happy and excited doing things and wearing things that I had not been able to wear or do before. It was the beginning of a new world for me. It was like being set free after living in a cage for years. Sadly, this only lasted for a season.

Little did I know, it was going to take more than that! It was only the beginning of a series of things that needed to change within me! Losing weight didn't solve all my problems. Yes, my health was much better, as a matter of fact, it was better than it had ever been before. I was able to walk a couple of miles without losing my breath, I couldn't remember the last time that happened. Doing simple things, like bending down and tying your shoes, crossing your legs, things you take for granted, I could do with no problem. But still, something important was missing.

I found myself sinking into a deep depression while looking like I was the happiest woman in the world. I did not know how I got there or how to get out. I really thought that I would be on top of the world after years of suffering with my weight. I lost enough weight to produce a whole person. But I found it harder and harder to get out of bed to be around people. I would get up angry and didn't know why, I wanted to sleep all day and to be left alone.

One of my problems was dealing with my body after the weight loss. I didn't weigh 450 pounds anymore, but I had all this loose skin hanging around. And let's just say, things didn't sit where they used to anymore. This created a different kind of problem for me. I didn't have the money to have the plastic surgery to remove the excess skin and to pull everything back into its proper place. With the depression settling in, I started to wear multiple girdles, I wore two bras at a time to keep my breasts up in the right place. I made jokes about them hanging down to my knees to keep myself from crying about it. Sometimes my clothes fit tight, people didn't understand it wasn't because I was trying to be sexy or anything, but the tight clothing held the skin together a lot better than loose clothing. Who wants to be jiggling all over the place when they walk? Not me. Most people are so quick to pass judgment without knowing your story or why you do or wear what you wear. And this too may be our fault sometimes because we're too private and not willing to share our stories.

Those issues took over my life and left me in a deep state of depression and loneliness. The feeling that I couldn't trust anyone to share my true story with invaded me. I feared what they'd think about me, how judgmental they'd be about the bad decisions that I've made in my life along with not forgiving myself and others. So, I held it all in and continued to die a little bit each day until now. My life started out with lies, abuse, deceitfulness, unforgiveness, obesity, and unhappiness. To make it plain, the sins of my parents - and myself - is how I got to that dark and desperate place. But God! My life is one of happiness, freedom, truth, salvation, and the best part of all - a relationship with the Lord. Because I'm desperate and determined, He thought I was worth saving, so Jesus paid for it, and I accepted it.

Chapter 4

What's My Name?

(He Knows My Name)

I am Victorene Foster. On December 21, 2019, I became Victorene Kellem. Finally married and the mother of five biological children and six stepchildren, the grandmother of twenty-six as of 2021. I have three sisters and five brothers. At my birth, my mother named me Victorene Johnson, though my last name should have been Ellis.

One might think, what's the big deal about your name? Everything! It was alright for my mother to give me my first and middle name (even though I do not have one). But the last name should have been given to me by the first man in my life - my father. It should only have been changed by the second most important man in my life, my husband. God created man as the head. The misplacement, and misnaming, meant my life began out of order and with a lie. Innocently and unintentionally, that misunderstanding of what's in a name caused things in my life to be out of alignment from my beginning. One of the first of many wrongs that I had no control over. This wasn't a positive way to start out in life. God placed man as the head for a reason and by removing him from his place of authority in our lives we throw our scales off balance. In the Bible, a man's name meant something, and it still does (or should) today.

Your name, represented your family, spoke of your character, your expected integrity, and your inheritance. A good name will take you places that money cannot buy you into! And keep you in places you cannot afford to stay! Even the world places value on your name, they call it a credit report. My name should connect me to my identity. My identity should link me to my family, my family should bring me into my inheritance, my inheritance to my expected character and integrity and all that leads to my destiny. The power of life and death are in our tongues according to The Word. So, what were they speaking over my life when they called me out of my name? And what have I continued to speak over myself? Was it life or death?

Destiny Nearly Aborted is the story of my life. How can I find my way if I don't know who I am? Can I be who I'm destined to be, without truth? Who am I really? I carried a name that I had no connection to. With no legal or blood ties, my first thought was I've lost my identity. But how could I lose something that I had never taken possession of? The identity that my mother gave me was wrong, but her mother gave her the wrong name too. My grandmother carried a name that didn't belong to her in my life, and she left this world with it. We all were living a lie. I don't know whether it was out of ignorance, or need, or fear. The need to belong and identify made me feel the need to continue the lie for myself. It was the same for them too! I don't know.

Bottom line: another generational curse that needed to be destroyed was passed on. Not to give your child their rightful name, is to take away their inheritance.

The name that I took on before December 21, 2019, belonged to my stepfather and he didn't give it to me legally. He was married to my mother at the time and didn't seem to mind. My older sister and I were the only ones who didn't have the Foster name. I wanted to look the part, to be a Foster like the rest of my family. Even as a child, the opinions of others were important to me. My mom and daddy and all the other kids had that name. Having a different name got in the way of being accepted as a part of my own family, so I thought. So often we want to look the part, because of what people might think or say. There were some in our family dynamics who would make a division and separate the children. I didn't want to be different or considered or referred to as a half-sister. Adults can be so inconsiderate when it comes to children's feelings. As if they didn't have any, and so can other kids. They would ask things like, "Why do you have different last names if that's your sister or brother?" That irritated me, we all had the same mother. I was young but had an older mindset, and I understood the division that was being placed in our family by others. I could really relate to that old saying, "Momma's baby and Daddy's maybe."

My mother had at least three kids before she was ever married. After she married my stepfather, who I always referred to as Daddy, he treated my sister and I like we were his own. Never at any time did he make us feel like he wasn't our father. It was other family members on both sides that did that! Why they felt the need to do such a cruel thing to children, I really wish I knew. But as I look back now, I can see that what he did was the most crucial factor in it all and not what others said or did. Anything we needed that Daddy could provide, he stepped up.

I remember when he and my mother were separated, Daddy was still there for us. I will never forget when I went into labor with my first child. Daddy called me in the hospital, asked if I was afraid, I told him yes. He said, "Hold on, I'm on my way." I laid the phone down and took a deep breath, and although I was still scared and in pain, I felt better knowing he was coming. He dropped everything for little old me. A child who did not have any of his DNA flowing through her veins, but one that he chose to make a personal commitment to, and he loved as his own.

Jesus did the same for us when He went to The Cross and gave His life for the sins of the world. We were all sinners; therefore, we were all separated from Him because of the sin. Even though we were separated, He still loved us so. He gave His life so that we might have a chance to choose to be reconnected to Him again. It was never about our blood; it's always been about the blood of Jesus that makes the difference.

He was coming from Arizona to be with me in California. Not just across town or down the street, but from state to state. Real daddies want to be there for their children no matter how young, old, happy, mad, right or wrong. It did not matter how far or what they must go through to get to them. My daddy didn't have much money. He received a state disability check, which wasn't even enough to take good care of himself. That man made a great sacrifice to get to me. My daddy, the one that I didn't have a right to, was there for me. I remember, I was in the third grade when I began to use Daddy's name. Family relationships are not just built on blood ties, but what you put into them. Jesus broke all the blood ties on The Cross.

Luther Foster was a wonderful father to me and a good husband to my mother. Yes, I can say good husband because my mother told me he was. She said the separation wasn't his fault; she was still a little "wild" back then. He was the one man who loved her unconditionally, besides God! I think in some way we are all looking for that special person who will love and accept us for who we are, whatever condition we are in. That one person who sees us naked, physically, emotionally, spiritually and mentally but will not run away. That person will still embrace us with love and encourage us to be the best version of ourselves possible in love. This is what Jesus did.

Daddy loved my mother so much that it made him love me too. Sometimes we can be blessed by association, and this was one of those times. Although we have no biological blood ties in common, he was still a father to me. Being a parent has nothing to do with your physical DNA. It did not matter that I did not carry any of his genetic information. I could still be a recipient of him. It was during the time of my son's birth that my mom and daddy decided to reconcile their marriage. Unfortunately, it didn't last long! Just six months after my son, Leon, and one month after the second grandchild, Clifford was born, Daddy passed away from a heart attack. My mother was devastated. She never fully recovered from it. He passed away right after a birthday party she had given him that weekend. On

Monday she found him. He was hanging half out of the bed onto the floor. A seizure caused the heart attack. My dad had epileptic seizures and as he got older, they became harder on his heart. That last seizure was one his poor heart couldn't take anymore.

Mom had been sleeping in the living room because she had broken her foot and had to sleep in a recliner with a cast on her foot. Daddy died in the early morning hours, and she never knew it, until late that morning. She blamed herself a lot, believing that if only she had only been in the room, she would have known, she could have called the ambulance and he could still be alive. There was nothing she could have done; it was his time. God is so good though, that He allowed him to come back to the woman he loved and his children to spend his last days. He was able to see two of his grandchildren born. By this time mom had another child, my youngest brother, who was four years old. Daddy treated him just like the rest of us, no difference.

Mom would get extremely depressed every year when it was Daddy's birthday. One day, about five years after his death, she suddenly started breaking dishes and yelling. She was angry with him for leaving her all alone. The pressure of life and loneliness were so overwhelming for her at that time. She thought about all the time she had wasted apart from him and now he was gone. You cannot understand the loss of a loved one until you experience it yourself. You lose a part of yourself with them many times over. No one will ever be able to take their place in your life or heart. I don't think you ever get over it altogether, but you can learn to live through your pain, with the Lord and good support in place.

I was blessed to have had a man like Luther Foster in my life. Although we had no blood or legal ties in common, we had something more important, a relationship. A relationship with your father is so important. There are things that only he is supposed to impart to you, whether you are a son or a daughter, it must come from the father. I knew he loved me as his daughter, and

I loved him as my father. But I took something, he didn't give me permission to have, and I had no right to! Because he loved me, he allowed it to be so. The Holy Father, and our natural fathers sometimes allow us to do things because they love us! They look beyond all our faults to see our needs. I needed to identify with a father figure. But I couldn't steal my identity, and I couldn't change who I was by changing my name, sooner or later my DNA ("The carrier of my genetic information, the fundamental and distinctive characteristics, the qualities of me, especially those regarded as unchangeable." – Webster's Dictionary). It was going to be tested and found not to be a match.

Chapter 5

DNA Connection

Your (DNA) identity will connect you to your inheritance. It gives you a blueprint of yourself. If you have a clear visual of your genetic history, you will be a better architect for the engineer. Every child, woman and man have a right to know who they are. Look! No matter how painful, how ugly or embarrassing the situation surrounding the conception of a child's birth, they have a right to know who and whose they are. The gift of life is never an accident or a mistake. God gives life and He alone. But we like to think we have control over who is born and who is not, but it is God who has the power to grant and take away life.

He doesn't have accidents and never makes mistakes. He (God) knew who your parents would be before you were ever conceived. He knew how and why before you were ever thought about! He knows what it will take for us to fulfill our purpose. He knows how much we can bear in every sense of the word. It takes some horrible situations to bring us to a place where God can use us for His glory.

Many of the Lord's most powerful men and women come from messed up situations. The kind of stuff where people don't want to know your name. They look down on you and at your situation as if you caused it to be so yourself. Most of them think that you will never be anything anyway. When you start to have problems with yourself, you will begin to think there is no hope. Those are the ones God wants, so He can get glory from their lives! Because only He can change you and me for the good. People make mistakes and accidents, but God is perfect. He is incapable of making mistakes or accidents.

My mother grew up without the knowledge of who her father was until later in life. It's not just about the name alone, but what comes along with it, the history, the inheritance! She had a right to know who her father was. Not just for herself, but for her family to come. I'm grateful to her for making sure her children knew who their fathers were, even though there were several of them. At one time that embarrassed me and made me ashamed of her. But now, I can see how much strength and courage it took not to have the wrong fathers around to save herself the embarrassment of the appearance of being a loose woman. She wasn't proud of having children by multiple men and some of them out of wedlock, but she was proud of her children. Although some of us may not have carried their last names, we did know who they were and as much history as she knew about them.

I was born October 3,1961, in Phoenix Arizona to Curtis Cain Ellis and Loretta Arletha Veronica Johnson. My mother began raising her children in a small town called Gila Bend, Arizona. It has been called one of the hottest spots in the nation, and that's not an exaggeration. By the time I was five we moved to California. Mom would continue moving us back and forth until I was about 11 years old. After that she would remained in Sacramento, California until her passing in 2012.

My sister Sandra and I were raised in our earlier years in the home of our maternal grandmother most of the time. We were the first grandchildren, and she was incredibly good to us. Momma was only 15 when Sandra was born and 16 when I came along. She was just a child herself and didn't seem to be quite ready to care for kids on her own, or so my grandmother thought. But Momma made sure we knew she was our mother. We were taught to always refer to her as Momma. But as time went on Momma decided that she wanted to care for her own children without interference. We moved to a one-bedroom cabin near my grandmother. But Momma wanted more for her children and herself than what one-bedroom cabin and small country town could offer. Not long after that she packed us up and moved to California. She would spend the next few years moving back and forth to California. Every time she would try to come back home it just didn't work out. So much unspoken stuff in that little place would fall out of closets. All the dirty little secrets nobody wanted to talk about or admit to were there.

Sandra and I would spend some summers with my grandmother. We would help around the house (more like a farm) with her animals. She enjoyed sitting in her yard with her water hose sprinkling the grounds and talking. I remember the smell of the water on the dirt ground when she would sprinkle it, it smelled so good. It made me want to eat the dirt. She would sit out there all day long. My grandmother had her own issues, but she was a good grandmother and I loved her unconditionally. When you love someone, you can see a person's shortcomings and see the best in them too!

One time my grandmother crocheted hats; she was really good at this. Sandra and I went door to door in town, trying to sell them. We were unsuccessful selling those hats. But we ran into an old Caucasian woman who wanted housework done. She was one of the well to do ladies around town. We talked with her and made an appointment for the following Saturday. We came on time, worked hard, and did an excellent job, at least that's what she said. At the end of the day, when it was time to be paid, she gave us a check for $3 and no cents! Can you believe that? We were not slaves! We may have been kids, but we knew that we had been severely underpaid. Not to mention she worked us like grown women. She should have paid us based on the work we did. My big sister had some words to say about that lady, that I will not repeat. I looked at her and took the check, smiled, and thanked her. As we were walking to the local grocery store to cash the check, we were talking to each other with great disappointment about how hard we worked for nothing. We got an idea to put a small zero next to the three. So, we did and received $30 instead of $3. When we got back to our grandmother's house, we showed her the money, she was so proud of us. She said, "she will call you back again." We knew that wasn't going to happen. We never told her what we had done to the check.

At another point in time, we also worked in the cotton fields for about a year. We earned about $250 a week together. We would cash our checks every week and give most of the money to our grandmother. Our grandmother was saving our money until it was time for us to go back home to California. Meanwhile, Momma was watching the news one day and saw how hot it was in Gila Bend. She immediately called my grandmother and asked her to send her babies home. By this time, the summer was over, and it was time to go back to school. Sandra and I were packing our things with great excitement about the money we had saved, it was about $1,500. That was like a million dollars to us. We planned to use the money to help our mother and buy more school clothes. Momma couldn't afford to buy us many clothes and we were starting high school for the first year. Well, as it was time to catch the bus, we went into our grandmothers' room to say goodbyes and collect our money. After small talk, Grandmother gave Sandra and I $50.00 together to take home and said how proud our mother was going to be of us. My mouth was wide open, I don't know if grandmother thought we couldn't count or what. WOW! We had worked so hard with that hot sun beaming down on us, again, this was not fair. Well, my sister said some words to me on that bus, that I will just leave on the bus. She would always have a word in times like that!

When we made it to California with our mother, we told her what had happened with Grandmother, she didn't seem surprised at all. Momma just said what a wonderful job we had done and tried to make us feel better by acting as if that $50 was the answer to her prayers. So, our grandmother was right about that, she was proud of what we had tried to do. We never spent another summer with Grandmother like that or worked in the cotton fields again. My mother would take us for short visits with her and the family; but never left us again.

Grandmother passed away since then and I miss her so much. I'm thankful to God I was able to tell her how much she had contributed to my life, and how much I loved her before her passing. I was thankful for giving her flowers while she could still smell them. Most of the time we wait too late to share our sentiments. Instead, at their homegoing service we make these grand speeches and say all kinds of wonderful, extraordinary things about them. We end up spending money we don't have and going into serious debt going to funerals when we have not seen or talked to the person in years. That seems so senseless to me. Once we are gone the words we articulate and the money we spend on the dead doesn't matter to the individual at all. Although my grandmother was not perfect and made mistakes, I loved her very much, and I made sure that she knew it.

As I think back, an old white woman we didn't know and an old black woman we did know, trusted, and loved, both took advantage of children. But the truth is, the check that we altered was wrong no matter the reason. It was not up to us to make it right. If we had left it alone, God would have taken care of her. Then the money that my grandmother didn't give us, I understood it to be a way of us paying back for what we did wrong with the altered check. Doing the wrong thing for what you might think to be the right reason, is still wrong!

Chapter 6

Trying to Understand Momma!

There are so many things that I didn't understand about my mother. Why she acted the way she did and why she was always trying to please her mother and others who were never going to be satisfied no matter what she did or gave them. At least that was the way it looked like to me. I swore that I would never be a people pleaser. No person deserves that much of you, that is reserved for God, Him alone!

One day with the passing of time, I realized that I was doing the same things she did. I also realized that I was incredibly angry with her too. I had been on a fast. I was praying, asking God to show me, me! And He let me know that I was angry with my mother. Well, I felt bad because I love my mother so much, and besides, she was dead now. How are you going to love and miss someone with whom you are angry? After I was done making excuses for why this wasn't or couldn't be true. I accepted the fact that God cannot lie, so it must be true. It wasn't until I started to trust him, He began to work on healing me of all the years of pain. Just because I had anger in me didn't mean I didn't love her; I just needed to admit it and forgive her and myself.

I too had bad relationships with the wrong men. Having a baby every other year. Looking all happy when I was really crying and dying inside. Just torn up from the floor up. I was becoming the mother that I never wanted to be. But what I failed to understand was that she was a part of me whether I wanted it or not. I saw so many imperfections in her, I wanted to be better. I saw her childish and irresponsible behavior. And there were times that I was embarrassed by that behavior. Unlike my mother, I grew up quick, too quick. Most of the time I felt like her mother, I think she felt like that too. I remember my mother coming home one night drunk, with no pants on. Don't know to this day where her pants were, and I never asked her. I just put her to bed and cried. What was she doing with her pants off? I don't know whether I cried because I was sad or mad. I didn't have much patience for foolish and childish behaviors. I didn't take into consideration her state of mind. Was she, herself, still a child in an adult body? What had she been through as a child herself and what price did she pay that kept the child inside her stunted when they should have grown up?

While there was still a child inside of her, she possessed a level of maturity that gave her a mind to keep all her children. A mindset to not give any of them away or flush them down the toilet, or let doctors suck the life out of her body, like milk from a straw. Like I did. I used abortions like birth control pills! How many did I have? I honestly don't remember; nor do I want to remember. Knowing I did such a horrible thing was more than enough for me, but God knows even if it were only one, it was one too many.

One time, I had come back from having an abortion, and I could tell from the expression on my mother's face, that she knew. Now it was her turn to be hurt, mad and ashamed of me. I had killed my own baby and her grandchild. The hurt in her eyes said everything as she fought back the tears. A few weeks went by, and while we were talking, she told me about children being a blessing. She never said anything to me directly about what I had done, but I got her point. I made a promise to myself that day, that I would never have another abortion again. I still grieve for the children I never got to meet.

It wasn't until January of 1997 that I began the process of forgiving myself for aborting my babies. Through the testimony of another young lady at church one night I began to face what I had done. She began to talk about what happened to her. God reached out and touched me that night and the process began. It's been a long and painful road, but a necessary one. Every chance I get to speak life to a woman or young girl I do! I will not let that experience be in vain! Although my mother had childish behaviors, she was woman enough to give birth to and raise all her children the best way she knew how; regardless of what society thought of her. There was an extraordinarily strong side to her as well as weak. She faced her life head on, and on her own terms. While I was trying so hard not to be like her, it made me weak in so many ways. What I saw as weakness, was actually strength.

Yes, my mother made a lot of mistakes along the way. But I can see that she was a strong woman in the end. Not running away from the unplanned events and situations in her life. Using what she knew and what was activated in her. Was there more in her? More than likely. But if you don't know how to awaken what's on the inside of you, what do you do? When you don't know who you are, or your capabilities and your self-worth, what do you do? I believe she did as much as possible with what she knew. I only wish I could let her know how proud I am of her. That's why it's so important that we give people their flowers now! She was so determined to not have her children grow up in that small town where she came from. A town where everybody was sleeping with the same old people.

Young girls didn't have a chance to have a relationship with a young man, because the older men were getting them. That's what she experienced. She wanted more for her children. She tried to teach us to love each other. What she thought love should be anyway. She said "You never fight your sister or brother; you fight for them. You don't talk about them to other people." Momma tried to stop the cycle that had been plaguing her family for so long. She was aware of the dysfunction of her mother and siblings, and even herself. But she didn't know what to do about it. She thought if she moved away from her family, it would solve the problem. But she couldn't or didn't understand that she was also a part of the problem! No matter where she went, the problem would still be there. She didn't understand that she had to deal with herself. Something in her was going to have to change, she was doing her best to make a change! Just because we are doing our best, doesn't mean that we should not try to do better! But she was working with missing information. Momma has passed on now, but I still need to carry on and make the necessary changes for our family to be free of this generational curse.

Chapter 7

About Me

After my last abortion, the Lord began to pull at my heart, and I started attending church again. Something in me was changing, I wanted a different way of life. One day the Lord touched my heart and I wanted Him. I needed to get out of the situation that I was in. I knew I couldn't serve God in it, and the Lord became the desire of my heart now. But the man, (father of my children) I was involved with wasn't willing to let me go that easy. Even though he really didn't want me anymore, he still wouldn't let go. It was the power and control over me that he liked. He forced me to have intercourse and I hated every minute of it. I feared what he would do if I said no. It would make me physically sick to have sex with him. I would go to the bathroom and throw up after a sexual encounter with him. I tried to wash the nasty feeling of it off my body, but that didn't help.

Then I found myself in the condition once again, pregnant. But it was different this time, not just because I made a promise to myself, and didn't tell anyone else about the promise, But God! He's tugging at my heart, my mind, my will. I wanted to do the right thing, and the wrong thing both at the same time. I was also concerned about what people would say about me. I heard what church people said about single women with multiple children and this was going to make number five for me. I wasn't married yet and had no plans to marry. "Who wants to marry a woman with all those kids? She needs to close her legs. She needs to stop having all these kids. Doesn't she know anything about birth control?" This was not an excuse in every case, but the saints needed to watch what they say to and about the younger and older women who find themselves in this condition. It's not always because of illicit or irresponsible behavior that pregnancy happens. Being abused, raped, and scared are reasons too. And you cannot tell this by looking at the kids they have or the maternity dress they're wearing. I could not do the mental abuse of the saints. I stopped going to church. I went back home and gave birth to my only daughter.

At that point, I was still in a forced relationship with their father. But the relationship for him was about control. It was sick! He did not want me, and I did not want him! He had other women on the side, the front, and the back. All I wanted, was to get back to my relationship with the Lord. But there was fear gripping my mind. I knew it was wrong to be in a relationship with my child's father, but I did not know how to get out? I thought God wanted nothing to do with me. But the Lord had not given up on me yet! God kept tugging at me. I started going to church again. The people at church were looking and talking about me behind my back, but I didn't care anymore. I had to come just as I was! Still in sin, but with a mind to want to change. I was still in that messed up relationship with the father of my last four children, a married man. Wrong, wrong, wrong! From the beginning, I was wrong to be in a relationship with him. This, however, didn't stop God's love from pulling at my heart. I became more distant in my relationship with my children's father and grew closer to the Lord. It was during that time I had to acknowledge the relationship between him and one of my sisters. That's right, my sister was one of the other women.

One day my sister got sick and was rushed to the hospital. Our mother went to the hospital to check in on her. When she arrived what she saw was heart breaking. She witnessed my sister and my children's father kissing in her hospital room. My mother hated him after that day. I actually had suspicions about their affair for a few years. But I didn't want to believe it. Who would want to? The pain that I felt inside once I faced the facts was unbearable. It was like something pulled my heart out of my body and twisted it until all the blood ran out. I wanted to die but couldn't. The thought of them being together made me sick to my stomach. How many times did he get out of my bed and go to her bed and vice versa? I became extremely depressed and withdrawn.

I was now ready to walk away from this part of my life. I needed God like never before. The father of my children wasn't having that. I was afraid for my life but didn't want to get other family members involved. I got myself into it and I had to get myself out. He was known to be a dangerous man in the streets. And whatever he wanted, he got. Through all of this I held on to God. But I came to a crossroad and had to decide, him, or God! One night I finally had the courage to take a stand for God!

He came over to my house. My father and children were asleep. He walked up to the door and had his gun in his pants pocket. I knew he planned to use it if I didn't cooperate with him. I had been putting him off and ignoring his calls. He didn't really want me; he just liked the feeling of having control and the power over me. Before his affair with my sister had come to light, he came over and raped me before. It was on a Saturday night. I went to church the next day and told my Pastors' wife. She was my friend; I don't think she really knew what to do or say to me at the time. She gave me some tissue and helped me clean my face as she tried to comfort and assure me that everything would be alright. It was after that I made up my mind that I wasn't going to give or allow my body to be taken and used by him again. I wasn't someone who was on the street, and it was time he stopped treating me that way. I deserved better from him. I was the mother of four of his children. And God deserved better from me, He had saved my life and my soul. He is worthy of the best that I have to offer.

So, when he returned this time, it was different, I was different, the fear that once had me, I now had it! When

I made up my mind, I was done being too afraid! God stepped in and gave me the courage to stand up to my giant. I told God that I was willing to die that night.

As he approached the door, I opened it before he could ring the doorbell. I didn't want him to wake my father or the children. He came in, and I sat down on the couch. I never had any intentions to go to my bedroom. I saw the gun hanging down in the pocket of his pants pulling them to one side. This time I wasn't afraid of him, I kept praying to God silently. So, he sat down beside me, we never said a word to each other all night. Next thing I know he's sleeping like a baby. I sat right there for hours while he slept, until he woke up and stumbled to the door as if he were drunk and climbed into his truck and drove away. I should have been concerned for his safety under the circumstances, but I was just relieved that he had left without any confrontations and never gave it a second thought. He never came back like that again and since then he has passed away. I was delivered from the fear of him that night, God did it.

As time went by, I found out that he had forced my sister to continue the relationship with him. He didn't force her to start it, just like he didn't force me to start, but he forced us to stay. She asked me to forgive her, and I did, and we are closer than ever. He also asked for forgiveness, and I did forgive him after much prayer. It wasn't an easy thing to do for me and it took time. I think the most difficult part of it all was the embarrassment of all the family and friends knowing what he did. Some may think that I deserve everything I got in the end. And maybe I did. I got Jesus in the end, and I didn't deserve that. I got delivered in the end, and I didn't deserve that. I got free in the end, and I didn't deserve that. I got forgiveness and I didn't deserve that. Praise God for getting what I didn't deserve in the end and for Him giving it to me despite sinful actions. The end results can be wonderful experiences when you get what you don't deserve!

It was only when I began to write this book, I realized I have been looking for a missing authority figure in my life to submit. The one person who will never leave me. Who will be strong when I'm weak and let me know everything is going to be alright, even when things look hopeless? Who accepts me just as I am flawed, broken, and often misunderstood? I've been looking for him not knowing the missing man in my life, has been there all the time! You know it was Jesus! He is the only one at this point that can bring total healing and deliverance to me. It would have been great to have that father figure full-time as a child, but I didn't, and I'm no longer a child anymore and it's time to stop operating as if I were one. I cannot turn back the hands of time in that way. The Bible says, in First Corinthians 13:11 "When I was a child, I spake as a child, I understood as a child, I though as a child: but when I became a man, I put away childish things" (KJV). It's time to mature and walk this out like an adult.

At the ripe old age of 50, I moved for the first time in my life to another state on my own. This was only because the Lord had given me a word that it was time to get out of Sacramento. He told me when and where. I was a little concerned about all the financial responsibilities that came along with that kind of move, especially out of state. The cost was going to be enormous for me, but I sought the Lord and He worked everything out. In 2011, two of my children and three of my grandchildren (whom I am the guardian for), moved to Salem, Oregon.

This was exciting and scary all at the same time, a new place, new adventure, new people, a new start! I was dependent on God for everything. This was a new season in my life, one He had spoken through someone not long before I left Sacramento. A prophet shared with me that God was going to restore the years the cankerworm had stolen. This was the beginning of that season. I had no idea how drastically my life would change. The new people that He was about to send in and the old ones He was about to remove would be pivotal. All I knew was, I was long overdue for a change!

When the Lord told me to go to Salem, I reached out to a cousin who lived there. I was as close to her as I could be to anyone. She loved me and reached out to help me make the transition as smooth as possible. I trusted her more than anyone I knew. We often talked and shared personal things, but I still had my guard up, unable to completely trust anyone. But as time went on, I trusted her more. I believe, the Lord brought me here, to deliver me from me! She was also there to help with the passing of my mother. That was one of the hardest experiences I've ever had. She was the first person that I talked with about my abuse as a child. The Lord was using her to begin my breaking point and release. I needed someone I could talk to that would not betray my trust, and she was it. God had started the process of His promise to restore me!

I will finish what my mother started but didn't know how to finish. I will awaken the woman in me! I will find my identity and walk in my destiny. It's time to help the little girl grow up and put away her dolls, say goodbye to her and hello to the woman. It's time for the woman to take charge and be accountable for her actions. The Lord has called me to speak truth, but before I can, I must face the truth in my own life first. It's time to face the fact that I killed some of my babies. I asked God to forgive me a long time ago, but I didn't forgive myself. I understand now if I don't forgive myself, I cannot move forward. It is time to deal with the molestation of the little girl and let her know that it was not and could never be her fault. The only ones to blame are the two grown men that took the body of a child and used it as if she were a woman! It's time to understand that I couldn't fix or save my mother. Only God could do that. It is time to forgive myself, so I can rest.

Forgiving yourself is the hardest part, even when it's not your fault. It is also one of the most powerful things you can do for yourself. You may think you are releasing others when you forgive, but it is you who is being unchained, receiving freedom and power. People move forward with their lives whether you forgive them or not. Believe that God will forgive you, and others can forgive you too. I choose to forgive them all. I choose to receive all my forgiveness of any and all deeds. I choose to receive my freedom from the chains of sexual abuse, lying, stealing, and killing my babies, the loss of my mother and anything else that has held me bound! I choose to never again be bound with the guilt, shame, and pain of my past - or future mistakes - for that matter. True repentance is why Christ died on The Cross so that I can have another chance, repeatedly. I choose to receive the power that Jesus Christ gave His life for me to have. Praise the Lord, I'm finally absolutely free.

My daughter, granddaughters, and every woman who will read these words; I want you to know that being a healthy woman takes demanding work and sometimes pain. Don't fear the pain, it only comes to bring healing and it will be well worth it. You my dears are worth it, all of it. Live in truth and be free and happy with yourself. Oh my God, how blessed you will be to realize you know who holds your past, present and future in His hands – God, The Father. When I made the right choice, the choice of me, the woman in me opened her eyes and awakened for the first time. I pray the same for you.

I pray that these 12 steps to freedom that I identified along my journey will lead you to your truthful and genuine victory.

#1 Disarm a lie by telling the truth; only truth can bring real freedom.

#2 Be truthful with yourself, then God, then others.

#3 If you are not honest with yourself, you will not be honest with anybody else, including God.

#4 Understand who you are. You cannot change what you don't know or understand.

#5 Accept and acknowledge who you are.

#6 Take back your identity. Find out which parts should remain and build on them. Whatever needs to be cast out and destroyed – release it! It is okay to be the best me!

#7 Take responsibility for your wrong doings(sins).

#8 Work on your flaws and weaknesses, with God you can overcome.

#9 Forgive others so that your Heavenly Father can forgive you.

#10 Forgive yourself in order to receive your power back.

#11 Seek God for total change and deliverance! Acknowledge that you need God to break every chain, and every generational curse over you, your family, and your friends!

#12 Know who and whose you are. Even when you don't feel or see it, keep believing it!

As a person of the Lord, I couldn't help anyone until I helped myself! I couldn't help myself until I faced my truth. Now I finally realize who I am. I will no longer settle for less than my value. I'm worth more than flaws and negativity. Jesus Christ paid too high of a price for me to be less than a conqueror. My attitude, my actions, my response, and my reactions to circumstances are affected by what I believe about myself. Your attitude isn't bad just because you don't feel good, or because you don't like someone, it's horrible because you don't like yourself. Your constant negative thinking about others and situations has to do with all the negativity you feel about yourself! Come on! It's time to deal with yourself and stop the hurt you feel inside. The hurting that is causing reproach against the body of Christ and those around you because you lack the manifestation of the best fruit (Galatians 5:22) in your life.

Don't let your destiny be aborted because you don't know your identity! Don't let your identity be a mystery because you're not willing to face and deal with yourself. When you place your life in the hands of Jesus Christ and you've completed the 12 steps to freedom, you will be, not can be, not should be, but will be free! It's the best thing you could ever do for yourself. Thank you for allowing me to share my story. I pray that it was a blessing to someone, and I pray that you find the freedom that I've found. I know it may be painful for you, but well worth it so that you can move forward in your life and receive all that God has for you.

My brother and my sister may God bless and keep you safe in His arms. I pray the Lord give you the strength to face every obstacle that the enemy has placed in your path that prevents you from moving forward. May you be transformed and freed by the truth of your identity in Jesus' name.

God, I pray this for every soul reading this testimony of Your glory. That they find and rest in their identity in You and that they rise from that place transformed. In Jesus' name, Amen.

ABOUT THE AUTHOR

Victorene Foster Kellem has a burning passion for empowering single unwed mothers. That passion comes from learning from lessons in her journey on that familiar road. This passion is the cornerstone of her ministry work to women. Second only to encouraging others to step toward transformation, instead of believing that it is too late to turn their life around, respecting self, and aspiring towards all your dreams. She has served as a Pastor's Aide for over 20 years, after beginning ministry work with the late Pastor Rickey A. Tates Sr. It was there that she became an evangelist before moving to Salem, Oregon. In Oregon, she would continue her pastoral administrative work, using her keen people skills, encouraging demeanor, dedication, and organizational skills to coordinate and manage congregational events.

After 25 years of service, God sent her the prefect mate in Apostle James E. Kellem of Detroit Michigan. With their union, she became the first lady of Dominion Covenant Fellowship of Churches International and the Supervisor of the Department of Women. Shortly after their marriage, Dominion Covenant Fellowship Church of Oregon was founded! She and her husband are a power couple for the Kingdom of God. Together they have eleven children and 26 grandchildren.

Destiny Nearly Aborted is her first book and chronicles her powerful story of breaking generational curses and making a conscious and intentional decision to change her life.

www.ingramcontent.com/pod-product-compliance
Lightning Source LLC
LaVergne TN
LVHW010453160826
845677LV00012B/2459

* 9 7 9 8 9 8 5 5 0 1 4 7 6 *